★ The ★
UNITED
STATES
PRESIDENTS

★ William H. ★
HARRISON

Heidi M.D. Elston

Big Buddy Books
An Imprint of Abdo Publishing
abdopublishing.com

abdopublishing.com

Published by Abdo Publishing, a division of ABDO, PO Box 398166, Minneapolis, Minnesota 55439.
Copyright © 2017 by Abdo Consulting Group, Inc. International copyrights reserved in all countries. No part of this book may be reproduced in any form without written permission from the publisher. Big Buddy Books™ is a trademark and logo of Abdo Publishing.

Printed in the United States of America, North Mankato, Minnesota
062016
092016

Design: Sarah DeYoung, Mighty Media, Inc.
Production: Mighty Media, Inc.
Editor: Lauren Kukla
Cover Photograph: Alamy
Interior Photographs: Alamy (p. 17); Corbis (pp. 5, 6, 7, 9, 27); Getty Images (pp. 7, 15, 23);
    Library of Congress (pp. 21, 29); North Wind (pp. 11, 19, 25); Picture History (p. 13)

Cataloging-in-Publication Data

Names: Elston, Heidi M.D., author.
Title: William H. Harrison / by Heidi M.D. Elston.
Description: Minneapolis, MN : Abdo Publishing, [2017] | Series: United States
    presidents | Includes bibliographical references and index.
Identifiers: LCCN 2015957542 | ISBN 9781680780987 (lib. bdg.) |
    ISBN 9781680775181 (ebook)
Subjects: LCSH: Harrison, William Henry, 1773-1841--Juvenile literature. |
    Presidents--United States--Biography--Juvenile literature. | United States--
    Politics and government--1841-1841--Juvenile literature.
Classification: DDC 973.5/8092 [B]--dc23
LC record available at http://lccn.loc.gov/2015957542

Contents

William H. Harrison

William H. Harrison was the ninth president of the United States. He served as president for just one month. This is the shortest time spent in office by any US president.

Harrison began his presidential term on March 4, 1841. At his **inauguration**, he caught a cold. He died one month later from **pneumonia**.

Harrison was president for a very short time. So, he did not have time to accomplish great things. But he still played an important role in American history.

Timeline

1773

On February 9, William Henry Harrison was born in Charles City County, Virginia.

1800

President John Adams made Harrison governor of the Indiana Territory.

1816

Harrison won election to the US House of **Representatives**.

1819

Harrison was elected an Ohio state senator.

1825

Harrison won election to the US Senate.

1836

Harrison lost the presidential election to Martin Van Buren.

1841

On March 4, Harrison became the ninth US president. William H. Harrison died on April 4.

Early Years

William Henry Harrison was born on February 9, 1773, in Charles City County, Virginia. His parents were Benjamin and Elizabeth Harrison. William's father was the governor of Virginia. William studied at home until 1787. Then, he went to college.

★ FAST FACTS ★

Born: February 9, 1773

Wife: Anna Symmes (1775–1864)

Children: 10

Political Party: Whig

Age at Inauguration: 68

Year Served: 1841

Vice President: John Tyler

Died: April 4, 1841, age 68

William spent his childhood at this house, which was on a large farm called Berkeley.

Moving West

In 1791, Harrison's father died. Harrison now had to get a job. That same year, he joined the military.

Harrison gathered 80 men. He led them to an area that is now Ohio. This area was part of the Northwest Territory. There, Harrison's men fought Native Americans for land.

In 1794, Harrison fought at the Battle of Fallen Timbers. There, the US Army won against Native Americans. Afterward, Harrison served as commander of Fort Washington in Ohio.

The Battle of Fallen Timbers ended fighting in the Northwest Territory. After the battle, Native Americans gave up claims to most of present-day Ohio.

Work and Family

While at Fort Washington in 1795, Harrison met Anna Symmes. She was well educated. The couple married that November.

The Harrisons had a long, happy marriage. They had six sons and four daughters. The family never had a lot of money. But they were close and loving.

In 1797, Harrison became an army captain. He left the military the following year. Then, he and his family settled on a farm at North Bend, Ohio.

The Harrison family home started as a four-room log cabin. Over time, Harrison added 12 more rooms!

Harrison enjoyed farming. But he needed more money to take care of his family. In June 1798, President John Adams made him **secretary** of the Northwest Territory.

In 1799, Harrison became the territory's first **delegate** to Congress. There, Harrison worked hard for Americans. People liked his ideas.

Harrison pushed Congress for the Land Act of 1800. This law split land into smaller pieces. This made it easier for poor settlers to buy land.

★ DID YOU KNOW? ★

Anna Harrison gave birth to the most children of any First Lady.

President John Adams

Governor Harrison

In 1800, the Northwest Territory was **divided** into the Ohio and Indiana territories. President Adams named Harrison the first governor of the Indiana Territory. Harrison served as governor for 12 years.

Governor Harrison tried to improve the well-being of the local Native Americans. He also made several **treaties** with Native American tribes. He gained many acres of their land in Indiana and Illinois for settlement.

While serving as governor of the Indiana Territory, Harrison and his family lived in this house in present-day Vincennes, Indiana.

Many Native Americans were upset about losing their land. So, they joined together under Shawnee Native American chief Tecumseh and his brother.

In 1811, Harrison led American troops into battle. They beat Tecumseh's men at Tippecanoe River in Indiana. The win earned Harrison the nickname "Old Tippecanoe."

Not long after, Harrison became commander of the Army of the Northwest. In the **War of 1812**, he won the Battle of the Thames. By winning this important battle, Harrison secured America's northwestern border.

The Battle of the Thames took place on the Thames River in Ontario, Canada. There, Harrison's men won against the British troops and the Native Americans who sided with them.

Working Hard

In 1814, Harrison once again left the military. However, he still wanted to serve his country. In 1816, Harrison won election to the US House of **Representatives**. He served until 1819. Then, he served as Ohio state senator until 1821.

In 1825, Harrison was elected to the US Senate. He served until 1828. That year, President John Quincy Adams made Harrison **minister** to Colombia. However, Andrew Jackson became president the next year. He sent a new minister to replace Harrison.

Harrison gained valuable experience during his time as a governor, a representative, a state senator, and a US senator.

Bid for President

In 1836, the **Whig Party** chose Harrison to run for president. However, the party also chose two other men to run. The **Democrats** chose Martin Van Buren.

Harrison did well in the election. But, he did not earn enough votes. Van Buren won the presidency.

Shortly after President Van Buren began his term, the Panic of 1837 struck. The nation suffered a **depression**. As a result, many Americans grew unhappy with Van Buren.

President Martin Van Buren

Another Campaign

The year 1840 brought another presidential election. Times were hard in the United States. Most people blamed the problems on President Van Buren.

Once again, the **Whig Party** chose Harrison to run for president. Harrison picked John Tyler as his **running mate**. Harrison ran against Van Buren.

Harrison campaigned hard. His **slogan** was "Tippecanoe and Tyler, Too!" Harrison's hard work paid off. He won the election!

A group of Whigs pushed a ball covered in Harrison slogans for hundreds of miles. This started the common saying, "Keep the ball rolling!"

A Short Term

On March 4, 1841, Harrison was **inaugurated** president of the United States. It was a windy, cold, and rainy day. Harrison caught a cold. Later that month, it turned into **pneumonia**. William H. Harrison died on April 4, 1841.

The US government was in a **challenging** position. Harrison was the first president to die in office. The US **Constitution** did not clearly say who should become president if the president died. So, Vice President Tyler named himself president.

President Harrison gave one of the longest inaugural speeches ever. He stood in the cold without a hat or a coat.

During his short time in office, President Harrison had named his **cabinet**. However, Tyler was a former **Democrat**. He still held Democratic beliefs. He disagreed with Harrison's cabinet on many issues. He **vetoed** many bills. So, all the cabinet members except one quit.

Harrison served the shortest presidency in American history. People believe he could have been a great president. William H. Harrison remains one of the nation's respected military leaders.

★ DID YOU KNOW? ★

William H. Harrison was the last US president to be born under British rule.

PRESIDENT HARRISON'S CABINET

March 4, 1841–April 4, 1841

- ★ **STATE:** Daniel Webster
- ★ **TREASURY:** Thomas Ewing
- ★ **WAR:** John Bell
- ★ **NAVY:** George Edmund Badger
- ★ **ATTORNEY GENERAL:** John Jordan Crittenden

Office of the President

Branches of Government

The US government has three branches. They are the executive, legislative, and judicial branches. Each branch has some power over the others. This is called a system of checks and balances.

★ Executive Branch

The executive branch enforces laws. It is made up of the president, the vice president, and the president's cabinet. The president represents the United States around the world. He or she also signs bills into law and leads the military.

★ Legislative Branch

The legislative branch makes laws, maintains the military, and regulates trade. It also has the power to declare war. This branch includes the Senate and the House of Representatives. Together, these two houses form Congress.

★ Judicial Branch

The judicial branch interprets laws. It is made up of district courts, courts of appeals, and the Supreme Court. District courts try cases. Sometimes people disagree with a trial's outcome. Then he or she may appeal. If a court of appeals supports the ruling, a person may appeal to the Supreme Court.

Qualifications for Office

To be president, a candidate must be at least 35 years old. The person must be a natural-born US citizen. He or she must also have lived in the United States for at least 14 years.

Electoral College

The US presidential election is an indirect election. Voters from each state choose electors. These electors represent their state in the Electoral College. Each elector has one electoral vote. Electors cast their vote for the candidate with the highest number of votes from people in their state. A candidate must receive the majority of Electoral College votes to win.

Term of Office

Each president may be elected to two four-year terms. The presidential election is held on the Tuesday after the first Monday in November. The president is sworn in on January 20 of the following year. At that time, he or she takes the oath of office.
It states:

> I do solemnly swear (or affirm) that I will faithfully execute the office of President of the United States, and will to the best of my ability, preserve, protect and defend the Constitution of the United States.

31

Line of Succession

The Presidential Succession Act of 1947 states who becomes president if the president cannot serve. The vice president is first in the line. Next are the Speaker of the House and the President Pro Tempore of the Senate. It may happen that none of these individuals is able to serve. Then the office falls to the president's cabinet members. They would take office in the order in which each department was created:

Secretary of State

Secretary of the Treasury

Secretary of Defense

Attorney General

Secretary of the Interior

Secretary of Agriculture

Secretary of Commerce

Secretary of Labor

Secretary of Health and Human Services

Secretary of Housing and Urban Development

Secretary of Transportation

Secretary of Energy

Secretary of Education

Secretary of Veterans Affairs

Secretary of Homeland Security

Benefits

★ While in office, the president receives a salary. It is $400,000 per year. He or she lives in the White House. The president also has 24-hour Secret Service protection.

★ The president may travel on a Boeing 747 jet. This special jet is called Air Force One. It can hold 70 passengers. It has kitchens, a dining room, sleeping areas, and more. Air Force One can fly halfway around the world before needing to refuel. It can even refuel in flight!

★ When the president travels by car, he or she uses Cadillac One. It is a Cadillac Deville that has been modified. The car has heavy armor and communications systems. The president may even take Cadillac One along when visiting other countries.

★ The president also travels on a helicopter. It is called Marine One. It may also be taken along when the president visits other countries.

★ Sometimes the president needs to get away with family and friends. Camp David is the official presidential retreat. It is located in Maryland. The US Navy maintains the retreat. The US Marine Corps keeps it secure. The camp offers swimming, tennis, golf, and hiking.

★ When the president leaves office, he or she receives lifetime Secret Service protection. He or she also receives a yearly pension of $203,700. The former president also receives money for office space, supplies, and staff.

PRESIDENTS AND THEIR TERMS

PRESIDENT	PARTY	TOOK OFFICE	LEFT OFFICE	TERMS SERVED	VICE PRESIDENT
George Washington	None	April 30, 1789	March 4, 1797	Two	John Adams
John Adams	Federalist	March 4, 1797	March 4, 1801	One	Thomas Jefferson
Thomas Jefferson	Democratic-Republican	March 4, 1801	March 4, 1809	Two	Aaron Burr, George Clinton
James Madison	Democratic-Republican	March 4, 1809	March 4, 1817	Two	George Clinton, Elbridge Gerry
James Monroe	Democratic-Republican	March 4, 1817	March 4, 1825	Two	Daniel D. Tompkins
John Quincy Adams	Democratic-Republican	March 4, 1825	March 4, 1829	One	John C. Calhoun
Andrew Jackson	Democrat	March 4, 1829	March 4, 1837	Two	John C. Calhoun, Martin Van Buren
Martin Van Buren	Democrat	March 4, 1837	March 4, 1841	One	Richard M. Johnson
William H. Harrison	Whig	March 4, 1841	April 4, 1841	Died During First Term	John Tyler
John Tyler	Whig	April 6, 1841	March 4, 1845	Completed Harrison's Term	Office Vacant
James K. Polk	Democrat	March 4, 1845	March 4, 1849	One	George M. Dallas
Zachary Taylor	Whig	March 5, 1849	July 9, 1850	Died During First Term	Millard Fillmore

PRESIDENT	PARTY	TOOK OFFICE	LEFT OFFICE	TERMS SERVED	VICE PRESIDENT
Millard Fillmore	Whig	July 10, 1850	March 4, 1853	Completed Taylor's Term	Office Vacant
Franklin Pierce	Democrat	March 4, 1853	March 4, 1857	One	William R.D. King
James Buchanan	Democrat	March 4, 1857	March 4, 1861	One	John C. Breckinridge
Abraham Lincoln	Republican	March 4, 1861	April 15, 1865	Served One Term, Died During Second Term	Hannibal Hamlin, Andrew Johnson
Andrew Johnson	Democrat	April 15, 1865	March 4, 1869	Completed Lincoln's Second Term	Office Vacant
Ulysses S. Grant	Republican	March 4, 1869	March 4, 1877	Two	Schuyler Colfax, Henry Wilson
Rutherford B. Hayes	Republican	March 3, 1877	March 4, 1881	One	William A. Wheeler
James A. Garfield	Republican	March 4, 1881	September 19, 1881	Died During First Term	Chester Arthur
Chester Arthur	Republican	September 20, 1881	March 4, 1885	Completed Garfield's Term	Office Vacant
Grover Cleveland	Democrat	March 4, 1885	March 4, 1889	One	Thomas A. Hendricks
Benjamin Harrison	Republican	March 4, 1889	March 4, 1893	One	Levi P. Morton
Grover Cleveland	Democrat	March 4, 1893	March 4, 1897	One	Adlai E. Stevenson
William McKinley	Republican	March 4, 1897	September 14, 1901	Served One Term, Died During Second Term	Garret A. Hobart, Theodore Roosevelt

PRESIDENT	PARTY	TOOK OFFICE	LEFT OFFICE	TERMS SERVED	VICE PRESIDENT
Theodore Roosevelt	Republican	September 14, 1901	March 4, 1909	Completed McKinley's Second Term, Served One Term	Office Vacant, Charles Fairbanks
William Taft	Republican	March 4, 1909	March 4, 1913	One	James S. Sherman
Woodrow Wilson	Democrat	March 4, 1913	March 4, 1921	Two	Thomas R. Marshall
Warren G. Harding	Republican	March 4, 1921	August 2, 1923	Died During First Term	Calvin Coolidge
Calvin Coolidge	Republican	August 3, 1923	March 4, 1929	Completed Harding's Term, Served One Term	Office Vacant, Charles Dawes
Herbert Hoover	Republican	March 4, 1929	March 4, 1933	One	Charles Curtis
Franklin D. Roosevelt	Democrat	March 4, 1933	April 12, 1945	Served Three Terms, Died During Fourth Term	John Nance Garner, Henry A. Wallace, Harry S. Truman
Harry S. Truman	Democrat	April 12, 1945	January 20, 1953	Completed Roosevelt's Fourth Term, Served One Term	Office Vacant, Alben Barkley
Dwight D. Eisenhower	Republican	January 20, 1953	January 20, 1961	Two	Richard Nixon
John F. Kennedy	Democrat	January 20, 1961	November 22, 1963	Died During First Term	Lyndon B. Johnson
Lyndon B. Johnson	Democrat	November 22, 1963	January 20, 1969	Completed Kennedy's Term, Served One Term	Office Vacant, Hubert H. Humphrey
Richard Nixon	Republican	January 20, 1969	August 9, 1974	Completed First Term, Resigned During Second Term	Spiro T. Agnew, Gerald Ford

PRESIDENT	PARTY	TOOK OFFICE	LEFT OFFICE	TERMS SERVED	VICE PRESIDENT
Gerald Ford	Republican	August 9, 1974	January 20, 1977	Completed Nixon's Second Term	Nelson A. Rockefeller
Jimmy Carter	Democrat	January 20, 1977	January 20, 1981	One	Walter Mondale
Ronald Reagan	Republican	January 20, 1981	January 20, 1989	Two	George H.W. Bush
George H.W. Bush	Republican	January 20, 1989	January 20, 1993	One	Dan Quayle
Bill Clinton	Democrat	January 20, 1993	January 20, 2001	Two	Al Gore
George W. Bush	Republican	January 20, 2001	January 20, 2009	Two	Dick Cheney
Barack Obama	Democrat	January 20, 2009	January 20, 2017	Two	Joe Biden

"Sound morals, religious liberty, and a just sense of religious responsibility are essentially connected with all true and lasting happiness." William H. Harrison

★ WRITE TO THE PRESIDENT ★

You may write to the president at:
The White House
1600 Pennsylvania Avenue NW
Washington, DC 20500

You may e-mail the president at:
comments@whitehouse.gov

37

Glossary

cabinet—a group of advisers chosen by the president to lead government departments.

challenge (CHA-luhnj)—something that tests one's strengths or abilities.

constitution (kahnt-stuh-TOO-shuhn)—the basic laws that govern a country or a state.

delegate—someone who represents other people at a meeting or in a lawmaking group.

Democrat—a member of the Democratic political party.

depression—a period of economic trouble when there is little buying or selling and many people are out of work.

divide—to separate into two parts.

inaugurate—to swear into a political office.

minister—a type of government official.

pneumonia—a serious disease that affects the lungs and makes it difficult to breathe.

representative—someone chosen in an election to act or speak for the people who voted for him or her.

running mate—someone running for vice president with another person running for president in an election.

secretary—an official chosen by the president to oversee something.

slogan—a word or a phrase used to express a position, a stand, or a goal.

treaty—an agreement made between two or more groups.

veto—the right of one member of a decision-making group to stop an action by the group. In the US government, the president can veto bills passed by Congress. But Congress can override the president's veto if two-thirds of its members vote to do so.

War of 1812—a war between the United States and England from 1812 to 1815.

Whig Party—a US political party active between 1834 and 1854.

★ WEBSITES ★

To learn more about the US Presidents, visit **booklinks.abdopublishing.com**. These links are routinely monitored and updated to provide the most current information available.

Index